Towards Understanding Surah Baqarah

Serena Hussain-Yates

Illustrations by Asif Mahmood

Copyright © 2020 by Serena Hussain-Yates

All rights reserved. No part of this book may be reproduced or used in any manner without written permission of the copyright owner except for the use of quotations in a book review.

Book design by Publishing Push
Illustrations by Asif Mahmood

ISBN Paperback: 978-1-914078-21-7
ISBN eBook: 978-1-914078-22-4

Published by PublishingPush.com

Dedication

I will like to dedicate this book to my late parents, Mohammed Hubdar Husain and Eva Husain

I will like to acknowledge my Brother Sahamadeen Hoosein whose story-telling, inspire me to write Chapter 5 using the concept of "The Flying Chair".

About the Author

Serena Hussain-Yates has been living in the United Kingdom for the last 36 years, having migrated from her native country Guyana.

A mother to four adult children and thirteen grandchildren, the author is the founder of BURTON SISTERS CIRCLE, a dawah giving organisation.

Contact details:
serenabibi@aol.com

Contact Details:
asif.designs@hotmail.com

Contents

Introduction vi

My Legacy vii

Chapter 1	The Sleepover 1
Chapter 2	Layla Went Back In Time 5
Chapter 3	The Adventures of Keyaan and Keystar 11
Chapter 4	Jasmine and the Story of the Cow 19
Chapter 5	The Adventures of Omari and Omaristar 27
Chapter 6	Nani Serena joined the Umah of Prophet Muhammad (PBUH) . . . 35

Introduction

This book tells the story of the adventure of four children and their Nani Serena. It traces the journey that they all experience in a dream. Each is accompanied by their own personal star that affords them to time travel. They are taken to live in the era of the different themes of the Surah.

Layla experience the creation of Prophet Aadam (AS) and death of Prophet Yaqcub (AS).

Keyaan went to Egypt and was there when Prophet Musa (AS) liberated the children of Israel. He then time travel to witness the miracles of Allah swt in the time of Prophet Uzairs (AS).

Jasmine always wanted to know where the name of the Surah, The Cow, came from. Her wish was granted when she was taken into that period to live the life of their people. Her desire to learn more about the world of the unseen was granted when she time travelled to live in the period of Prophet Sulaiman (AS).

Then Omari's interest in giants came though when his star took him on a flying chair to see the battle of Prophet David (AS) and Goliath.

In the final chapter Nani Serena lived the time of the second Migration where she joined the Ummah of Prophet Muhammed (AS) in Medina.

Comprehension of Surah Baqarah is incumbent of all Muslims and its of utmost importance that this understanding comes from an early age.

Using this theme of time travelling will captivate the young readers and experiencing the lives of the people of their time will form lasting understanding of the Surah.

My Legacy

My children,

My grandchildren,

I leave this book as a legacy to you. In this journey of life Allah has chosen me to be your guardian, your protector. Allah has entrusted me, gifted me with the best of treasures, my beautiful family.

Live your life in the submission and affirmation to the one God.

All that exists belongs to Him as He is the Originator of all. He, subhanahu, alone is worthy of worship and all other deities are to be shunned.

Everything happens by the Qader (will) of subhanahu. What was never meant for you will never reach you and what is meant for you, you will never have missed.

Live your life with kindness, gratitude. Live everyday as the last day of your life. Seek refuge in Allah from the accursed Shaitan who lies waiting to trap you.

Fulfil your duties to one another. You might be four different families but live your life as one. There is nothing greater than kinship.

Remember that happiness comes with a pure heart free from jealousy, hatred, arrogance.

Establish your prayers regularly and with humility. Nothing in your life is more important than your Salaat. Prayer is your connection to Allah.

Feel the hunger and thirst of others. Thank Allah in all conditions. He may know a thing that's good for and that what is bad.

Learn the lessons from the Prophets. Put your trust in Allah and avoid those who aim to cause mischief. Speak well of others and avoid slander and backbiting.

Live your life with contentment and avoid excess. Have pleasure in giving than receiving.

Be charitable to your neighbours and love for yourself what you love for your brother. Live your life with tolerance and be accepting of others, even if their beliefs differ from you.

Ask forgiveness from those you harm and repent to Allah.

I pray that Allah protect and guide each and everyone one of you and we meet again and live as one family in Jannatul Firdous.

AMEEN
Mummy, Nani Serena.

CHAPTER 1

The Sleepover

Layla, Keyaan, Jasmine and Omari are having a sleep over with Nani Serena. They wore their best pyjamas for this occasion and brought along their favourite teddies. They settled themselves into bed patiently waiting for Nani to tell them the story of Surah Baqarah.

Nani started her story- telling.

Surah Baqarah is the second chapter of the holy quran. It is also the longest surah and our Prophet Muhammed (PBUH) tells us:

"Recite the Qur'an, for on the Day of Resurrection it will come as an intercessor for those who recite It. Recite the Two Bright Ones, al-Baqarah and Surah Al 'Imran, for on the Day of Resurrection they will come as two clouds or two shades, or two flocks of birds in ranks, pleading for those who recite them. Recite Surah al-Baqara, for to take recourse to it is a blessing and to give it up is a cause of grief, and the magicians cannot confront it." (Muslim 804)

"Surah Baqarah has many stories in it and tonight children, I will tell you some of these stories", Nani Serena explained.

The children were getting drowsy as Nani finally finished her storytelling.

As the they were nodding off, something magical starting happening.

They were no longer in their beds.

The Sleepover

With hands joined Nani Serena and her grandchildren were travelling into space. The night was crystal clear. The moon was shinning in all its glory. The twinkling stars dancing for joy to welcome Nani Serena and the children into their hemisphere.

"What's happening Guys?

"Look over there!", Keyaan said pointing to set of exceptionally large stars.

These stars seem to be travelling at great speed towards these homosaphians.

"They have arms and it looks like they are reaching out to us", Layla said with great excitement.

"Wait up, wait up", screamed Jasmine. It looks like they have our names.

The words can hardly come out of Omari's mouth when he shrieked pointing towards the stars:

"That one says Omaristar, that's his name, that's his name, that's my star," Omari kept on repeating.

As the stars are getting closer all the names became recognisable.

Serenastar extended her arms to Nani, and with a firm grip took her to Planet Jupiter. Jupiter is the largest planet in the solar system.

Omaristar got hold of Omari's hands. They travelled towards a large orange-red star. It was Planet Mars.

Jazzistar moved towards Jasmine and journeyed towards Planet Venus, the second brightest natural object in the night sky.

Keystar approached Keyaan with great speed, whipped him to the second largest planet in the solar system, Saturn.

By this time Layla was left alone floating around the universe.

Excitement overcame fear as she gazed at the majestic beauty of the vast expanse of the universe.

She was caught unaware when Laystar came and gently took her hand. She could not believe her eyes when she was taken to the moon. That was her wish.

Suddenly, a voice although sweet and gentle thundered through the universe, bringing all the children and Nani to attention.

It was Serenestar.

She was addressing everyone. She told that in the beginning there was just one ball in the universe. There was no sun, no moon, no stars. This ball, because of the intense heat, grew larger and larger, until there was a big explosion with lots of smoke.

And the solar system was formed from this occurrence.

Allah then created seven heavens one above the other.

She then went on to talk about **Surah Baqarah.**

She tells them that the surah contains many rules on a variety of topics guiding us how to live on this earth. It explains why Allah created jinns and mankind and what will happen when we die.

She went on to say that Allah sent many prophets to deliver these messages and Surah Baqarah contains information about most of these prophets and the times they lived in.

Serenestar then put a proposal out and asked if everyone would like their Star to take them back in time so they can receive these messages with the people of those era.

Nani Serena and her grandchildren could not believe what they were hearing and shouted their agreement in chorus.

Each gave an account of which time they would like to be transported to.

Nani Serena wanted to be taken back in time to the Ummah of the Holy Prophet Muhammed (PBUH) after his second Hijrah to Medina.

Layla chose to visit the time when Prophet Aadam (PBUH) was created in the lower heaven.

Keyaan wanted to time travel in the era of Pharaoh and Prophet Musa (PBUH).

Jasmine wanted to find out why the Surah was called Surah Baqarah (The Cow) and asked her star to take her to that period.

Omari is going to live in the era of Prophet Dawood (PBUH) and Jalut.

CHAPTER 2

Layla Went Back In Time

"Hop on Layla", Laystar beckoned.

Layla could not believe her eyes and asked:

"Can I sit on you, Laystar, like Alladin did his on the magic carpet"?

Laystar intended just that. Layla positioned herself in the middle of her Star.

And the magic began.

From the points of Laystar grew shimmering tiny wings. Layla once again found herself in the galaxy.

She was on cloud nine. Her Star was moving at enormous speed.

Laystar has many friends in the universe and there were so many kisses and salaams blown to them as they travelled along. Heaven was an awfully long way from the moon and this journey will certainly be a remarkably interesting one.

The earth that seemed so big appeared just as a tiny ball from that distance in space. There were many balls in the universe. Some larger than others. Laystar explained that these were the planets and that they all rotate around the sun. Layla can observe this phenomenon.

It was spectacular.

They have been traveling for awhile when they arrive at a large golden gate with its keeper.

"And who might you be", roared the gatekeeper.

In a very meek and sweet voice, Laystar gave her reply:

"I am Laystar and I have brought Layla, a human from earth. She is a time traveller".

In a split of a second the gate opened.

What awaits Layla was nothing she had seen before.

The gate gave way to a path that was paved with gold dust, and it took them to four palatial buildings.

Layla knew she must be in the lower heavens.

She could not believe her eyes when she saw four palaces. They all had names:

The Yates Family

The Arshad Family

The Mahmood Family

The Qadir Family

Laystar told Layla that those were the palaces built for her family in Jannah. However, they must live according to Allah's rules to gain their entries. If they do not, then they will live in the fire of hell.

She told her that Allah swt tells us in **Chapter 13, verse 23 to 24** about this:

23. Gardens of perpetual bliss: they shall enter there, as well as the righteous among their fathers, their spouses, and their offspring: and angels shall enter unto them from every gate (with the salutation):

24. "Peace unto you for that ye persevered in patience! Now how excellent is the final home!"

Laystar told Layla that there is a someone who will try to mislead her to the hellfire and with this she read the following verses from **Surah Baqarah: 24-25**

24. But if ye cannot- and of a surety ye cannot- then fear the Fire whose fuel is men and stones,- which is prepared for those who reject Faith.

25. But give glad tidings to those who believe and work righteousness, that their portion is Gardens, beneath which rivers flow. Every time they are fed with fruits therefrom, they say: "Why, this is what we were fed with before," for they are given things in similitude; and they have therein companions pure (and holy); and they abide therein (for ever).

Layla then hopped on to her Star to witness the story of the creation of Prophet Aadam (AS).

They entered a blissful garden with luscious greenery and beautiful flowing springs.

There were luminous flying beings carrying baskets of soil. Laystar explained that these were angels sent to parts of the world to collect different shades of soil. These soil Allah swt used to create the first human being.

They then flew to another part of the garden and the created being stood there. He was gigantic. He was 60 cubits tall. The average human is only four to five cubits.

Then Layla saw the one who will try to take the descendants of Prophet Aadam(AS) to the hellfire, Iblis.

He was staring at the innate Aadam. Without life he stood in that spot for 40 years. Iblis was insanely jealous of Aadam and knew he was created for great things.

Layla then witnessed a ball of light travelling towards Aadam. It was Allah swt giving him a soul. When it reached Aadam's head, he sneezed.

The angels said: "Say all praise belongs to Allah." Adam repeated:

"All praise belongs to Allah."

Allah said to him:

"Your Lord has granted you mercy."

When the spirit reached his eyes, Aadam looked at the fruits of Paradise.

When it reached his abdomen, Adam felt an appetite for the food. He jumped hurriedly before the spirit could reach his legs, so that he could eat the fruits of Paradise.

Allah, therefore, said: *"Man is created of haste."* [Al-Quran 21:37]

Layla is about to witness a replay of Iblis's disobedience.

When Allah asked the Angels and Iblis to prostrate to Aadam(AS) Iblis refused Allah's commands.

He felt he was better. That made him the first racist, thinking he is better because he was created from fire and our father Prophet Aadam (AS) was created from soil.

It was then Allah made him an outcast. He was to live in the hellfire forever. But he asked Allah to grant him special powers. He wanted to mislead all the children of Aadam and take them with him to the hellfire.

He was granted that power, but Allah told him that he will never be able to mislead those who believe in him.

Layla now understood what she will be up against when she retuned to Earth. She felt that she must keep the memory of the Palaces she saw. She also knew that it would be her obligation to tell everyone how easy they can be misled if they don't follow guidance from Allah swt.

Layla was then to see Prophet Aadam's wife, Hawa.

Allah also created her. All humans came from Prophet Aadam (AS) and Hawa. That is what makes all humans part of a brotherhood, regardless of their status, appearances, wealth, and beliefs.

Allah swt told Prophet Aadam(AS) and his wife to live happily in Paradise. Allah swt gave them his permission to eat everything except the fruits from a particular tree. This was going to be their first test. Man faces many tests and trials and only following Allah's rules can help to overcome them.

Then it all happened.

Iblis is now going to use his special powers. He whispered to Prophet Aadam (AS) and his wife Hawa to eat the fruits from the forbidden tree.

They forgot about Allah's rules and did exactly what Iblis want. However, unlike Iblis they were deeply sorry and begged Allah for forgiveness. Allah forgave them but ordered that they too must leave heaven to live on Earth.

Layla knew that her journey has ended, and she must now return to earth. She asked Laystar if she can be granted one more wish.

"What is your wish, Layla? Her Star asked.

Layla wanted to be taken to the time of Prophet Yaqcub (AS).

The kind Laystar granted her wish and soon they were traversing again. She has never travelled in the daylight before. The sky was the bluest she has ever seen, with the golden sun in all its might and glory, guiding its visitors. The beautiful clusters of drifting clouds seem to be calling out to Layla.

Next thing Layla and her Star takes up comfortable position on a large blanket of moving clouds.

By this time Layla felt confident hopping on and off her star. Infront of her there was a beautiful family of clouds all motioning to her to join them. She soon finds herself cloud hopping. Other clouds in the sky seem to be gravitating closer to observe Layla's new skill.

But alas!! All good things must come to an end.

After saying their goodbyes, Laystar and Layla slipped away from their newfound friends.

They are now starting to make their descent.

They have arrived.

They were in Egypt. Laystar's mission was now to find the dying Prophet Yaqcub (AS).

They were flying for awhile.

And there it was.

A re-created scene of the time Prophet Yaqcub (AS) died.

There was the frail old man on his deathbed, surrounded by his twelve sons. He was giving a speech. He was most concerned that after his death his children might forget the essence of true worship.

Prophet Yaqcub (AS) lived his life re-enforcing the message to worship one God free from partners, and on his deathbed continue to advise his children to the teachings of Islam, the religion of all of God's prophet.

Prophet Yaqcub (AS) closed his eyes and slipped away a happy man, reassured that his legacy will carry on.

Surah Baqarah tells us:

"And this was the legacy that Abraham left to his sons, and so did Jacob; "Oh my sons! Allah hath chosen the Faith for you; then die not except in the Faith of Islam." **(Verse 132)**

This was indeed an emotional situation for Layla, and with outstretched arms Laystar circled her little protégé. She lifted her up to a sitting position on her making their way back.

Layla had another surprise. They were not returning to Earth, but to the moon.

Laystar has developed a sort of fondness for Layla. Laystar who lived with her family on the moon invited her to stop with her to await her nanny and cousins.

The Adventures of Keyaan and Keystar

CHAPTER 3

Keyaan was happily playing with Keystar's siblings on Planet Saturn. He did not even realise that his Star was not around. The young stars were most impressed by the numbers of surahs Keyaan can recite. They looked in awe as the child started reciting verses 49 to 64 from Surah Baqarah. Those verses were about Prophet Musa saving the Bani Israel.

Then as if from nowhere Keystar appeared.

Keyaan shrieked in delight. His star was sitting in an orange car and was motioning the young child to take up position in the driver's seat. That car is like the one Keyaan has in his garden in Planet Earth.

The next thing, they were speeding along in the beautiful blue sky. They are now going to Egypt.

Keyaan's wish is finally coming through. He will be able to witness the enactment of Prophet Musa crossing the Red Sea and life at the other side.

Keyaan love his adventure. At one point his Star had to tell him off as he was driving at such great speed colliding with the clouds.

As daylight is giving way to darkness Keyaan knew he will be arriving soon at his destination.

And there it was.

It was early morning.

Prophet Musa (AS) and his brother Prophet Haroon (AS) were leading the Bani Israel out of Egypt. Pursuing them were the army of Pharaoh.

There was sheer terror on the faces of the unfortunate people. Infront of them was the turbulent Red Sea and behind were the army of galloping horses, in pursuit at enormous speed.

They were trapped

These were people that had seen so many miracles and they have full faith that Allah will not let them suffer.

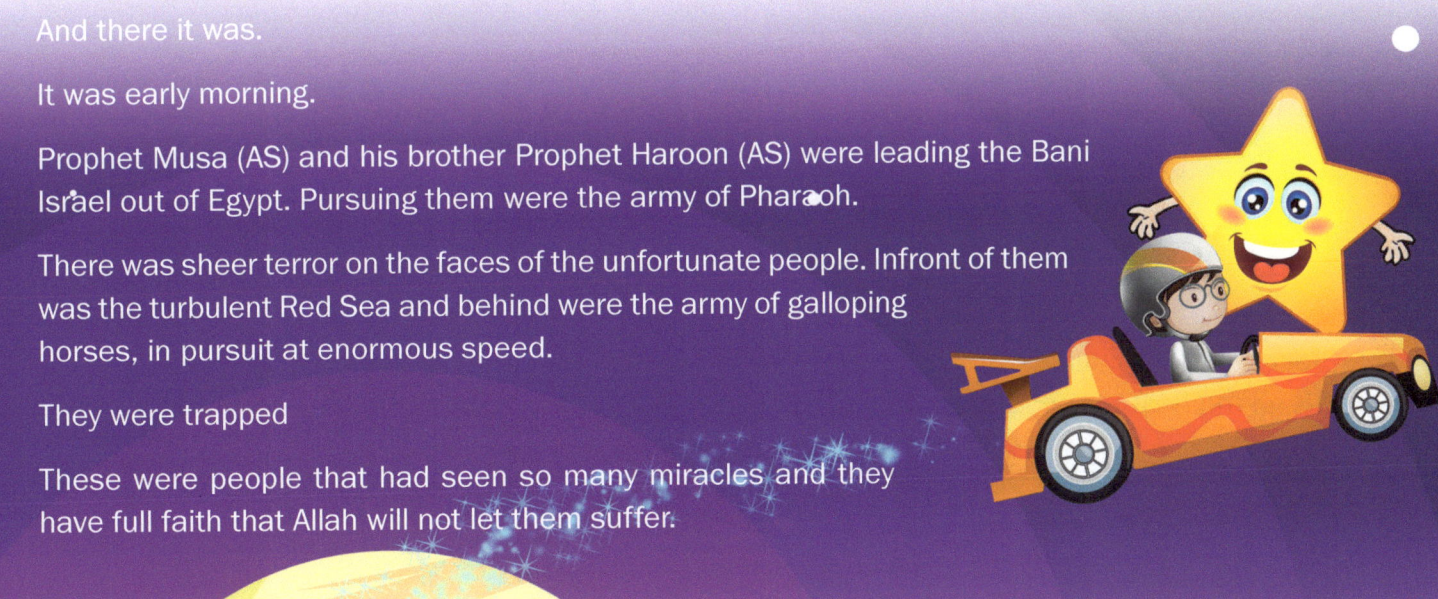

There were men, women, and children. There were pregnant women, there were feeble old men. Keyaan wished he could help some of the children by transporting them in his car. Keystar had to remind him that his experience was not real, and he was in a world of dreamland and what he was witnessing is a re-creation.

Even upon hearing that the Young Keyaan was experiencing the emotions of the refugees.

Then it happened.

Prophet Musa (AS) used his staff and strike the Red Sea.

It parted.

The dry seabed appeared with the torrential waves either side.

As Prophet Musa (AS) and his brother Haroon (AS) were leading the children Keyaan and his Star were zooming across honking their horns.

Then relief once again turned to fear as Pharaoh and his army were trying to use the same path to reach them.

Then the miracle happened.

The sea started closing in.

The water was reaching Pharaoh's neck when he started shouting:

"I believe in the God of Musa and Haroon".

But it was too late, and the waves enveloped him, and he was no more.

Everyone was now safe and sound at the other side of the Red Sea.

As can be expected the people were hungry and thirsty. Their journey was long and difficult, and the heat was scorching.

Keyaan wanted to join the people. His Star told him to hop off. He stretched his arms and legs and were running around amongst the children.

There was a young man waving to him.

With a shocked face Keyaan asked:

"Can you see me"?

Keyaan couldn't believe his eyes when the young boy said he could see both him and his Star.

He introduced himself as Yusha.

Keyaan decided it will be so cool to hang around with someone who had lived 9000 years ago.

"I don't ever want to wake up", Keyaan excitedly told Keystar.

The intense heat turned to coolness as overhead clouds were shading them.

Yusha then alerted Keyaan to observe what Prophet Musa (AS) was doing.

The Prophet used his staff to strike the ground and twelve springs appeared. Each of the twelve tribes of the Bani Israel were to have their own spring.

Another miracle was yet to come.

From the sky came Manna and Quails.

Allah was indeed kind to the Children of Israel.

Keystar whispered to Keyaan to look out for the ungratefulness of the Children of Israel.

Keyaan responded that he knows that they will be dis- satisfied with Allah's mercies and will ask for lentils and onions.

No sooner than those words were said the people were addressing Prophet Musa (AS) with that request. The prophet scolded them.

But the biggest shock was when they wanted to copy some idolaters they met. Some of the Bani Israel thought it would be a good idea for them to also engage in idol worshipping.

The prophet was most displeased and reminded them of the miracles they had witnessed from the one true God.

By now keyaan was very eager to have a chat with Yusha.

"Hey Yusha", keyaan called out, "were you the boy who was with Prophet Musa (AS) when he went looking for Kidr , and were you later granted Prophethood?.

With a huge grin Yusha disappointed Keyaan when he replied that he was not.

The Adventures of Keyaan and Keystar

Keystar told Keyaan that something important was going to take place. Prophet Musa was going to be commanded by Allah swt to go to Mount Sinai for 30 days to receive revelations from Allah swt.

"You are going to see what will happen now in the absence of Prophet Musa (AS)", Keystar said to Keyaan.

Yusha also joined in the conversation, expressing that he was also keen to find out.

Keystar pointed to an individual name Samiri. He was an evil man and suggested they find another God as Prophet Musa has broken his promise by not returning after 30 days. Allah told him to fast an extra ten days.

Samiri addressed all the people to give him their gold jewelleries. He told them that he was going to make a living God.

The people were split. Some rejected him whilst others obliged and gave him all their jewelleries.

Prophet Haroon (AS) who the prophet left in charge was helpless. He cannot stop Samiri or dissuade his followers.

Keyaan watched as Samiri built a big fire and threw all the gold in it. He then pretended as if he was performing magic and threw some dust in the fire.

From the molten metal he shaped a golden calf. It was hollow, and the wind passing through it produced a sound. Since superstition was imbedded in their past, they quickly linked the strange sound to something supernatural, as if it were a living god. Some of them accepted the golden calf as their god.

At a distance Keyaan could see Prophet Musa(AS) approaching.

"Phew, I wondered what's going to happen now", he thought silently.

The prophet was carrying two tablets. The revelations were written on them.

What a site awaits him.

The people were singing and dancing around the calf statue

The Prophet was furious. He flung the tablet and severely reprimanded the idolaters. Even Prophet Haroon (AS) felt his anger. But he subsided when he realised that his brother was helpless in the situation.

Keyaan cannot wait to see what punishment was going to be dished out now.

The prophet banished Samiri into exile and told the others to repent for their actions.

Prophet Musa (AS) chose seventy elders to accompany him to Mount Sinai. He ordered that they must repent for their idolatrous actions.

Keyaan and his Star jumped in his car and sped along with them.

The elders heard Prophet Musa speaking with Allah swt. Keyaan could not believe his eyes when he heard the elders demanding to see Allah. Their arrogance was soon to be rewarded.

With punishment!

They were punished with lightning bolts and violent quaking of the earth.

The seventy elders lay dead.

Prophet Musa's heart was filled with sorrow and begged Allah swt to forgive and revive them.

They all then came back to life.

Keyaan was eager to spend some time with his friend Yusha. With Keystar he drove his car to find him.

Yusha had many questions for Keyaan about life in the twenty first century. Keyaan told him about the other two prophets after their Prophet Musa (AS)

His direct words were:

"Yusha, in your time you follow the message sent to Prophet Musa (AS). There were many other prophets afterwards. Some of them were killed by your people.

There was another prophet called Prophet Isa (AS). He brought the same message as your prophet. Your people in our time are called Jews. They did not believe that he was the true messiah. They are still waiting for him. The people that follow him are called Christians and they thought he was one of three – Allah, Allah's son and the holy ghost. Quite confusing you see. Then Allah sent one last prophet to deliver his message to all the people and to correct the misbeliefs of your people and the Christians.

I am from that time and the Prophet was Prophet Muhammad, may peace and blessings of Allah be upon him. I am a Muslim and my religion is Islam".

With that eloquent speech Keyaan hugged Yusha and extend an invitation for him to visit him in his world.

"Hey Keyaan", Keystar shouted, "I can grant you another wish. Is there somewhere else you will like to go?"

Indeed, Keyaan was in no hurry to return to earth and asked if they could visit the time that Prophet Uzairs (AS) lived.

They were off on their travels again.

Oh no! They were caught in a rainstorm. The rain kept pelting down. Keyaan absolutely loved the heavenly downpour. Switching on his wipers he was having the time of his life.

Then appeared a beautiful arc in the sky. It was the rainbow with its all defined colours. Keyaan drove his car through touching each of the colours.

As they were descending, Keyaan was able to see the large expanse of golden soil beneath.

As they were getting closer, they saw a young man riding his donkey.

"That's your man", Keystar said to Keyaan. "That's Prophet Uzair".

Drenched in sweat Keyaan could sense his discomfort. He must have been quite hungry because the next thing he did was to sit under the nearby Kaiber tree and started eating.

The view infront of him was one of ruins.

"Keyaan, look at those", Keystar alerting the young traveller to what seems a bed of skeletal bones.

By the look on Prophet Uzair's face he was also shocked at seeing them and wondered how could Allah brought all this back to life.

Then Keyaan saw it all happened.

Keyaan saw the miracle.

Allah then sent the angel of death to take the prophet's life. And he lay dead for one hundred years.

His donkey also died during this period.

Allah then brought the prophet and his donkey back to life. Prophet Uzairs understood then that Allah is all mighty and nothing is impossible for our creator.

Keyaan is once again back in the universe with Keystar driving his car. It was a beautiful stary night. Keystar help Keyaan steered his car so he can see all the planets. They were all smiling at him blowing kisses.

Eventually they arrive at Keystar's home to await his Nani to take him back to Planet earth.

Jasmine and the Story of the Cow

CHAPTER 4

A big surprise awaits Jasmine in Planet Venus. Her favourite pink unicorn toy was there. But the difference this time is that its real. She was flapping her shimmery wings and with a big grin on her face she lifts her hoof up as if to say:

"Nice to see you Jasmine."

Jazzystar with an even bigger grin addressed Jasmine:

"Do you like your surprise"?

Jasmine had no time to reply and just jumped on her Unicorn. Jazzystar joined her.

And they are off on their travels.

The sky was alight that night. It seems like all the starts in the universe have come out to welcome Jasmine.

And that is exactly what was happening. Her planet Venus has arranged this welcoming party.

And there was yet to be another surprise. Jazzystar is going to recite Ayaltul Khursi.

It was a heart rendering recital and all the stars were making duas during this recital.

255. Allah. There is no god but He,-the Living, the Self-subsisting, Eternal. No slumber can seize Him nor sleep. His are all things in the heavens and on earth. Who is there can intercede in His presence except as He permitteth? He knoweth what (appeareth to His creatures as) before or after or behind them. Nor shall they compass aught of His knowledge except as He willeth. His Throne doth extend over the heavens and the earth, and He feeleth no fatigue in guarding and preserving them for He is the Most High, the Supreme (in glory).

Jasmine blew kisses to the stars and with her companion, Jazzistar, mounted the Unicorn and started her journey.

The Journey was long but exciting and finally darkness gave rise to daybreak.

There is no doubt about it. They were in another time zone.

"Descend", Jazzistar said to the Unicorn.

As the Unicorn makes it descent, they found themselves amongst people who were in complete chaos.

These were the Bani Israel. The time frame was after the exodus from Egypt and after Prophet Musa's (AS) visit from Mount Sinai.

People were on opposite sides of a corpse debating.

Jaazistar suggested that they dismount the unicorn and move closer.

"This pointing of fingers isn't solving the problem of who committed this murder", said a wise old man.

"We should really take this matter to Prophet Musa (AS), said another.

At the headside of the deceased there was a man going overboard with his crying.

"That's the nephew", Jazzistar informed Jasmine.

Jazzistar told Jasmine that the deceased was very wealthy and had no children and his death seemed to hit the nephew quite hard.

By now news of this incident reached the attention of Prophet Musa (AS). He prayed to Allah swt.

The Bani Israel got their answer.

Allah inspired the prophet to tell them to slaughter a cow, and this will lead them to the killer.

Jasmine could not believe her ears at the questions they were posing to the prophet:

"Are you making fun of us"?

"Are you taking us in mockery and jest"?

"What possible connection can there be between a man who was killed and sacrificing a cow"?

They thought that the decision of Allah swt did not correspond with their concern.

Prophet Musa responded:

"Allah swt forbid that I should be among the foolish!"

They wanted Allah swt to be more specific

The Prophet clarified,

Towards Understanding Surah Baqarah

"It should be a handsome yellow cow."

They once again asked Prophet Musa for more information.

"Because all cows look the same to them".

Jasmine surprised her Star by reciting the verses from Surah Baqarah about this incident.

"Call on your Lord for us," they said, "that He might inform us what kind she should be."

"Neither old nor young says God, but of age in between," answered Moses. "So do as you are bid."

"Call on your Lord," they said, "to tell us the colour of the cow."

"God says," answered Moses, "a fawn coloured cow, rich yellow, well pleasing to the eye."

"Call on your Lord," they said, "to name its variety, as cows are all alike to us. If God wills we shall be guided aright."

And Moses said: "He says it's a cow unyoked, nor worn out by ploughing or watering the fields, one in good shape with no mark or blemish."

"Now have you brought us the truth," they said; -[2:67-71]

By now Jasmine decided to do a bit of exploring. With Jazzistar, her Unicorn is taking them further afield. It was a glorious day.

They came to a field and there was a young man with a cow.

"Hang on!!! That cow seemed to match Prophet Musa's description", Jasmine told her Star.

"Look ahead Jasmine, there are the Jews", Jazzistar reponded.

The Jews were out searching for the cow.

"Hey, look at that one", said one of the Jew pointing to the heifer. "That's it, that's our cow", he continued.

So they went one to approach the young boy. He had just lost his father and the cow was his only inheritance. He lived a humble life with his poor mum. He was a very dutiful son.

"Will you sell your cow to us"? they asked him.

The youth told them that he will have to consult with his mother. They all accompanied him to his house.

"We will offer you three gold coins for your cow", one of them proposed to his mom.

Jasmine and the Story of the Cow

"Oh, no, no, no. My cow is worth a lot more than three gold coins", she replied.

They went on increasing their offer and the mother kept on refusing. Finally, they urged the son to speak to his mother to be reasonable.

He told them:

"I will not sell the cow without my mother's approval, even if you offered me its skin filled with gold!"

On hearing this, his mother smiled and said:

"Let that be the price: its skin filled with gold."

They realised that no other cow would do; they had to have it at any price. They agreed to buy the cow and paid the price.

They took the cow to the prophet.

The scene was now intense. The slaughter was done. They took a chunk of the animal and touched the dead man with it.

Jasmine held her breath.

"I can't wait to find out who the murderer is", she muttered beneath her breath.

Then the miracle happened!!!

The corpse came back to life.

He looked around and studied everyone. He then turned back and the wailing nephew, still at his headside was identified as the murderer.

It was time for Jasmine to leave. However, she will not be returning to earth yet. Jazzistar will take her to Babylon to witness another re-created scene from Surah Baqarah.

She was going to experience an incident that happened at the time of Prophet Sulaiman (AS).

Jasmine In Babylon.

Jasmine is now setting off to visit the ancient city of Babylon. Unicorn spread her shimmery wings, rose in the sky and off they went.

There were lots of flying jinns in the sky that night. Some of them are very disobedient and follow the footsteps of Shaitan.

Before the revelation of the Quran they used to ascend towards the lower heavens to eavesdrop on discussions between angels and then pass the information on with a hundred lies to the magicians.

However, after the Quran came down, the angels will shoot them, and we perceive the fallen jinns as shooting stars.

There were many of them in the sky that night.

"Wow, there are many eavesdroppers tonight" Jasmine conclude as she gazed at the magnitude of shooting stars.

Alas! Their journey is coming to an end.

The ancient city of Babylon is now in sight.

The huge buildings and statues surrounded with walls of ancient writings gave the visitors of the time zone they are in.

As Unicorn was descending many strange beings were in sight.

Jasmine knew instantly that these were the Jinns.

Although, Jinns were normally invisible to humans, in this instance because Jasmine is in dreamland these beings became visible.

They were all busy at work. Some were constructing, some were making cauldrons and pots. It was indeed a remarkably busy site.

Some of the Jinns were even chained in cages.

They were all under the command of Prophet Sulaiman (AS). He was indeed blessed with many miracles. He also understood the language of the birds and ants and could control the winds.

There was a figure of a man leaning on a stick watching the Jinns hard at work.

"That's Prophet Sulaiman (AS)" Jazzistar informed Jasmine.

But something did not feel right about this situation. The prophet was very still and appeared not to be breathing.

"Jasmine, the prophet is dead and had been dead for awhile", told Jazzistar.

One can conclude from that scenario that the Jinns do not know the unseen as they were none the wiser that the Prophet was deceased.

Infact, the discovery was made by a human of the prophet's death. Jasmine watched the scene intently as he was carried away for his burial.

Jasmine and her companions then flew into the palace. She wanted to see the interior.

It was spectacular. The floors were made of glass and beneath it were running water. The walls were of cedar panels overlaid with gold. There were elaborate carvings, golden lampstands, bronze pillars, ivory doors and large silver windows.

The Prophet's throne was huge and under it was a large chest. This chest contains books of magic used from information passed on to the magicians from the Jinns. Before the coming of Prophet Sulaiman (AS) the Bani Israel practiced the art of magic. Engaging in magic is a very grave sin in Islam.

Hence, Prophet Sulaiman (AS) seized all these books, stored them in the chest and kept it under his throne. Any attempt made to retrieve these writings were met with grave punishment. The prophet proclaimed he will burn the jinns and behead humans if found guilty of this act.

Then another scene unfolded.

Jasmine, her Star and Unicorn were to experience a remarkably interesting incident.

There an individual who was leading a group of people to the Chest.

He appointed himself as the spokesperson.

He was telling the people:

"O people! Sulaiman was not a prophet; he was only a sorcerer! Go and seek his sorcery in his dwellings and luggage."

He led the people to the chest. They removed all the books and the practice of magic started all over again.

From that point onwards, the false news that Prophet Sulaiman (AS) was a magician spread amongst the people. This was indeed a great injustice.

Jasmine at that point felt that she needed a break.

Jazzistar suggested that they explore the garden. Off they went circling the majestic garden. Its beauty was breathtaking. There were multistoried terraces with the most attractive hanging baskets. There were springs and fountains with gushing water.

Leaving this beautiful site, they decided to fly further afield.

They eventually came to a large gathering of people. Two men were addressing the crowd.

Jazzistar told Jasmine that this scene is explaining Verse 102-103 from Surah Baqarah.

102-103:

"They followed what the Shayatin (devils) gave out (falsely of the magic) in the lifetime of Suleiman (Solomon). Suleiman did not disbelieve, but the Shayatin (devils) disbelieved, teaching men magic and such things that came down at Babylon to the two Angels, Harut and Marut, but neither of these two (Angels) taught anyone (such things) till they had said, "We are only for trial, so disbelieve not (by learning this magic from us)." And from these (Angels) people learn that by which they cause separation between man and his wife, but they could not thus harm anyone except by Allah's Leave."

The men addressing the crowd were Angels sent by Allah swt. Their names were Harut and Marut.

Harut and Marut's role were to teach the children of Israel the difference between miracles and magic.

Allah defended the prophet saying that the prophet never practiced magic and by the permission of Allah he was blessed with miracles.

"It was the devils who were the disbelievers and not the Prophet".

They were also sent as a test to distinguish the believers from the non-believers.

The Angels warned them of this and of the consequences if they used their information to indulge in sorcery.

Some heed the advice whilst others became disbelievers by using magic to split families.

Jasmine's visit has finally come to an end. She now fully understood where the name Baqarah came from.

She was mesmerised by the city of Babylon with all its mysteries and supernatural happenings. She is well and ready to return to Planet Venus to await her Nani.

The journey back was a pleasant one. Jasmine was totally unaware of the happenings in the universe. She was in deep thought reflecting on her remarkable experience.

And there they were. Finally, in Venus amongst the family of Jazzistar, wondering what further experiences she will have.

The Adventures of Omari and Omaristar

CHAPTER 5

"Omari, Omari", Omaristar's voice echoed in the vast expanse of the universe.

"Look what I have for you".

Omari could not contain his excitement and squealed:

"That is my chair, that's my favourite chair, and it has wings. It's my Mari".

Omaristar surprised the little Omari by bringing his favourite chair, Mari. However, it was somewhat different. Spurting out from each side there was a pair of large wings. Mari also now has a face and two long arms. For sure he looks so different now.

With the biggest of smiles Mari, the chair said:

"I guess you are surprised to see me Omari. I will be joining you on your adventure."

This is certainly a dream Omari never wants to wake up from.

Without any hesitation, Omari joined hands with Omaristar, hopped onto Mari and the adventure began.

A journey in the sky is nothing like Omari has experienced before.

Mari:

"Omari, I have never told you before, but you are my best friend. I will be your chair forever. This is the first of many journeys".

Omari was too busy marvelling at the beauty of the universe to even acknowledge Mari's admission.

All of Omaristar's friends with came to join then. What a wonder sight it was with all the Stars flying alongside Mari and his occupants.

They surprised Omari by reciting verses:

Surah Al Baqara verse 246-251:

Have you not thought about the group of the Children of Israel after (the time of) Musa (Moses)? When they said to a Prophet of theirs, "Appoint for us a king and we will fight in Allah's Way." He said, "Would you then refrain from fighting, if fighting was prescribed for you?" They said, "Why

The Adventures of Omari and Omaristar

should we not fight in Allah's Way while we have been driven out of our homes and our children (families have been taken as captives)?" But when fighting was ordered for them, they turned away, all except a few of them. And Allah is All-Aware of the Zalimun (polytheists and wrong-doers). Prophet Samuel (AS) prayed to Allah, and Saul (Talut) was appointed their king. Saul set out with a big army, but his army was infiltrated by hypocrites. When the army was passing a river, King Saul wanted to test his soldiers and so he told them to only drink from the hollow of their hands, and not to fill their bellies. The Quran says in Al-Baqarah 2:249: Then when Talut (Saul) set out with the army, he said: "Verily! Allah will try you by a river. So whoever drinks thereof, he is not of me, and whoever tastes it not, he is of me, except him who takes (thereof) in the hollow of his hand." Yet, they drank thereof, all, except a few of them. So when he had crossed it (the river), he and those who believed with him, they said: "We have no power this day against Jalut (Goliath) and his hosts." But those who knew with certainty that they were to meet their Lord, said: "How often a small group overcame a mighty host by Allah's Leave?" And Allah is with As-Sabirin (the patient ones, etc.).

"Looks like we are here lad", said Omaristar.

They have reached their destination.

Mari made a smooth landing. Omari and his star jumped off whilst Mari parked himself under a nearby tree.

In a distance there were a large crowd of people. Omaristar took hold of Omari's hand and they flew to the scene.

The crowd was being addressed by Prophet Shamill (Samuel) . The country was without a king and everyone of high status were there. Each hoping they will be the chosen one.

"Hey Omaristar, Omari addressed his star, "can you take me flying"?

With that request Omaristar gently held the child's hand and they rose. The sky seems saturated with the most beautiful plumages. They belong to the flocks of exotic birds that were flying with them.

Their synchronizing singing reminds one of the magnificence of Allah's creation.

Along a muddy path they saw two young boys in conversation. One of them seemed very worried and the other was reassuring him.

"We will find your donkey, Talut".

Talut (Saul) lived in a farm with his father and with his servant they are searching for his lost donkey.

Talut:

"I really feel we should return home. Father will be worried about us".

The servant:

"I heard that Prophet Shamill lives close by. Let's go and ask him if he knows where our donkey is".

With that Mari let out a laugh and thought it would be a good idea to follow them.

"Mari, where did you come from? We left you under the tree", exclaimed a surprised Omari.

"Never you mind. I will soon return to being just your chair and I am not going to miss out on anything", the cheeky Mari told his best friend Omari.

"They cannot see us you know Omari", Omaristar said gleefully.

But Omari already knew that. That is what makes their journey so exciting.

They asked a group of passers-by to direct them to the Prophet's house.

They arrived feeling so tired. Talut wiped the sweat off his forehead as he looked for a place to sit.

The prophet saw him and bekonned:

"You, young lad, come forward".

Young Talut ran to him. The prophet placed his hand on his head and declared:

"This is your new King. This is going to be your new ruler. He will lead you in battle to fight the Philistines and return our Arc of Convenant".

The crowd was shocked, but not as shocked as Talut.

"I am no king. I am just a shepherd who has lost a donkey", responded Talut.

The crowd agreed with Talut and have their own statements to add:

"That Talut is just a lowly person", one prominent member of the community spoke.

"He is from the Benyamin tribe", spoke another.

"He doesn't have any wealth", another joined in.

And the negative comments kept pouring in.

However, Prophet Shamil was undeterred and said that he was following the signs of Allah and that Talut is the next King of Israel.

The Adventures of Omari and Omaristar

That decision was final and no amount of protest was going to change it. It was the decree of Allah swt that Talut was going to be the New King.

Talut's first job was to start preparing his army for battle. They must fight the Philistines and win back their Arc of Covenant.

Mari, Omaristar and Omari were at the scene when Talut was recruiting his army.

He said to the people:

"I do not want the following category of people to join my army:

Those of you who are building homes,

Who recently got married,

Who are engaged in business affairs".

King Talut was very wise and needed full concentration of his soldiers.

The trio are now witnessing the strenuous training Talut is putting his army through.

Omari was overly impressed by all of this and said:

"Think I would like to be a soldier when I am a grown up".

Omaristar and Omari made themselves comfortable sitting on Mari and off they went following the army.

Talut addressed his army:

"We will now come to the River Jordan. Can I advise, those of you who are thirsty, please drink just sips of water".

Omari sitting on his flying chair could not believe what the people were doing and blurted out:

"Stop people, stop gulping down the water

The king was extremely disappointed and dismissed the greedy ones.

He needed his people to be sincere.

During the journey he put his army through many more tests and by the time they reached the land of the Philistines, there were only 30 soldiers remaining.

Their journey was a long one and arrived after several days.

And there it was! The battle scene!

The Philistines' army was huge. The soldiers were well equipped with their weapons.

The opposition was just a small army, but they had complete faith in Allah.

The giantlike Jalut fronted his army and roared to the opposing soldiers:

"I challenged anyone of you to a single combat".

In those days, rather than the whole army fighting, it was their custom to send one soldier from each side to fight with each other.

Jalut's huge stature scared the soldiers from King Talut's army and no one took up the challenge.

By this time King Talut was getting quite desperate and pleaded with his army:

"I offer my daughter's hand in marriage to any soldier who dared face Jalut".

Then to everyone's amazement, a young lean looking man stepped forward. He was Dawud (David).

The Adventures of Omari and Omaristar

"I will fight you Jalut", he said.

"Oh no, no, you wouldn't youngman", a disappointed Talut responded. "Do you have any experience"?

Dawood replied:

"Not really, I have only come here to watch the battle, and my father told me just to be a standby. But I have killed a tiger and lion before".

Talut admired young Dawood's courage but felt that he was no match for the strong giantlike Jalut.

Seeing the desperation on the King's face, Omari asked Mari to do something to save the situation.

"Omari, you know we are not real, and this is a -recreated scene, we can't help", Mari said.

But there is more to come that cause the young Omari to be even more anxious.

"Haha, look at you against me. I will cut your head off with one blow", screamed the giant to the young boy.

But the courageous Dawood was not afraid and replied:

"I have strong faith in Allah and I am not afraid of you".

The scene was now beginning to get tense. Dawood set forth with a slingshot, he wheeled a stone and hurled it at Jalut.

Omari gasped as the stone hit Jalut. It hit him straight on the head and Jalut fell down. He was lifeless.

Jalut's army was very shocked to see their great general killed by a little boy and they ran away, but the army of King Shamill killed them, and they became victorious.

"They won; they won the battle. Now they will have their Arc of Covenant returned to them", squeeled Omari.

"Did the king keep his promise and let Dawood marry his daughter?" Omari asked his star?

"He sure did, and also Dawood was granted prophethood", replied Omaristar.

Omari's adventure has now ended and has to make his way back to his Planet.

He held his Star's hand, and they both hopped on to Mari.

Their journey back was beautiful and the universe was filled with renditions of Surah Baqarah 243-251. Young Omari joined in with the recitals:

247. Wa qaala lahum Nabiy yuhum innal laaha qad ba'asa lakum Taaloota malikaa; qaalooo annaa yakoonu lahul mulku 'alainaa wa nahnu ahaqqu bilmulki minhu wa lam yu'ta sa'atamminal maal; qaala innallaahas tafaahu 'alaikum wa zaadahoo bastatan fil'ilmi waljismi wallaahu yu'tee mulkahoo mai yashaaa'; wallaahu Waasi'un 'Aleem

248. Wa qaala lahum Nabiyyuhum inna Aayata mulkiheee ai yaatiyakumut Taabootu feehi sakeenatummir Rabbikum wa baqiyyatummimmaa taraka Aalu Moosa wa Aalu Haaroona tahmiluhul malaaa'ikah; inna fee zaalika la Aayatal lakum in kuntum mu'mineen

249. Falammaa fasala Taalootu biljunoodi qaala innal laaha mubtaleekum binaharin faman shariba minhu falaisa minnee wa mallam yat'amhu fa innahoo minneee illaa manigh tarafa ghurfatam biyadih; fashariboo minhu illaa qaleelamminhum; falammaa jaawazahoo huwa wallazeena aamanoo ma'ahoo qaaloo laa taaqata lanal yawma bi Jaaloota wa junoodih; qaalallazeena yazunnoona annahum mulaaqul laahi kam min fi'atin qaleelatin ghalabat fi'atan kaseeratam bi iznil laah; wallaahuma'as saabireen

250. Wa lammaa barazoo liJaaloota wa junoodihee qaaloo Rabbanaaa afrigh 'alainaa sabranw wa sabbit aqdaamanaa wansurnaa 'alal qawmil kaafireen

Fahazamoohum bi iznillaahi wa qatala Daawoodu jaaloota wa aataahul laahulmulka Wal Hikmata wa 'allamahoo mimmaa yashaaa'; wa law laa daf'ullaahin naasa ba'dahum biba'dil lafasadatil ardu wa laakinnal laaha zoo fadlin 'alal'aalameen

247. Their Prophet said to them: "(Allah) hath appointed Talut as king over you." They said: "How can he exercise authority over us when we are better fitted than he to exercise authority, and he is not even gifted, with wealth in abundance?" He said: "(Allah) hath Chosen him above you, and hath gifted him abundantly with knowledge and bodily prowess: Allah Granteth His authority to whom He pleaseth. Allah careth for all, and He knoweth all things."

248. And (further) their Prophet said to them: "A Sign of his authority is that there shall come to you the Ark of the covenant, with (an assurance) therein of security from your Lord, and the relics left by the family of Moses and the family of Aaron, carried by angels. In this is a symbol for you if ye indeed have faith."

249. When Talut set forth with the armies, he said: "(Allah) will test you at the stream: if any drinks of its water, He goes not with my army: Only those who taste not of it go with me: A mere sip out of the hand is excused." but they all drank of it, except a few. When they crossed the river,- He and the faithful ones with him,- they said: "This day We cannot cope with Goliath and his forces." but those who were convinced that they must meet Allah, said: "How oft, by Allah's will, Hath a small force vanquished a big one? Allah is with those who steadfastly persevere."

250. When they advanced to meet Goliath and his forces, they prayed: "Our Lord! Pour out constancy on us and make our steps firm: Help us against those that reject faith."

251. By Allah's will they routed them; and David slew Goliath; and Allah gave him power and wisdom and taught him whatever (else) He willed. And did not Allah Check one set of people by means of another, the earth would indeed be full of mischief: But Allah is full of bounty to all the worlds.

Nani Serena joined the Umah of Prophet Muhammad (PBUH)

CHAPTER 6

Nani found herself in the city of Yathrib, now called Medina. She was amongst a large gathering of people who were rejoicing, beating drums and singing a melodious tune. Nani seemed to recognise this tune and started singing along.

Tala al Badru 'Alayna
Min Thaniyati-al Wada'
Wajaba Shukru 'Alayna
Ma da'a lillahi da'

O the white moon rose over us
From the valley of Wada'
And we owe it to show gratefulness
Where the call is to Allah..

Nani was aware that she looked, dressed, and spoke differently from the people there. However, Serenestar reassured that she was invisible. She was a time traveller, and no one can see or hear her.

Upon hearing this, Nani Serena ran to the front of the crowd.

It was then she saw the man on the camel approaching the crowd. He was the most beautiful human being she has ever seen.

She knew that this must be the last and seal of all prophets, Prophet Mohammed (saw).

This was the second migration. The holy prophet and his companion, Abu Bakr were coming from Mecca.

Nani Serena knew that there were different groups of people living in Medina. She read it in Surah Baqarah. She wanted to visit them.

Serenestar gave Nani some clarity on these categories of people. They were the believers, the non- believers and the hypocrites. She further went on to say that until the day of judgement these types of people will populate the world. Serenestar advised Nani Serena that she must follow the guidance of the Quran and be amongst the believers.

Nani Serena visiting the three categories of people living in Medina

In the twinkling of an eye Serenestar and Nani Serena found themselves amongst a large group of people. They were in dikr praising Allah swt.

The hills were echoing their melodious tunes.

What a wonderful sight. With hands opened, eyes closed, these believers were making their spiritual connections to their creator, Allah swt.

Serenestar explained that Surah Baqarah describe them as people with Taqwah, with Imaan and these are the people who will benefit from the Quran. They are very true and sincere, and they believe that which cannot be seen nor proven and know that their knowledge is limited and Allah's knowledge is infinite. They have complete faith and submit totally to the one who gave them life.

They were the believers.

Nani Serena understood then why her Star tells her that she must strive to be in this category of people.

Next, they travelled to meet another group of people.

They were in what appeared to be a large field with lots of idols and statues. The people there were prostrating to these man-made creations. They did not believe at that time in the message of Islam.

Surah Baqarah tells us that these are the people who have the faculty of hearing and seeing but they wilfully made themselves blind by choosing to cover their eyes and ears, and these are the people who will not benefit from the message of the Quran.

Finally, they are going to visit the hypocrites.

This would be quite interesting as Nani thought many people in the world fall into this category.

They find themselves in a marketplace with many people.

The hypocrites were amongst them.

Sereneastar told Nani Serena what Surah Baqarah says about these people.

"They are known as those who say they believe, but secretly they are not among the believers. They only mock".

They are being described like those who are in darkness. The darkness of their own desires, the darkness of evil. They are aware of the situation. They want a way out and seek to find the right path. They are given that path of light, but they ignore it, and because of this Allah calls them:

Summum bukmun 'umyun fahum laa yarji'oon

(Deaf, dumb and blind, and so they do not think and understand).

Allah has blocked their guidance and they will not benefit from the Quran.

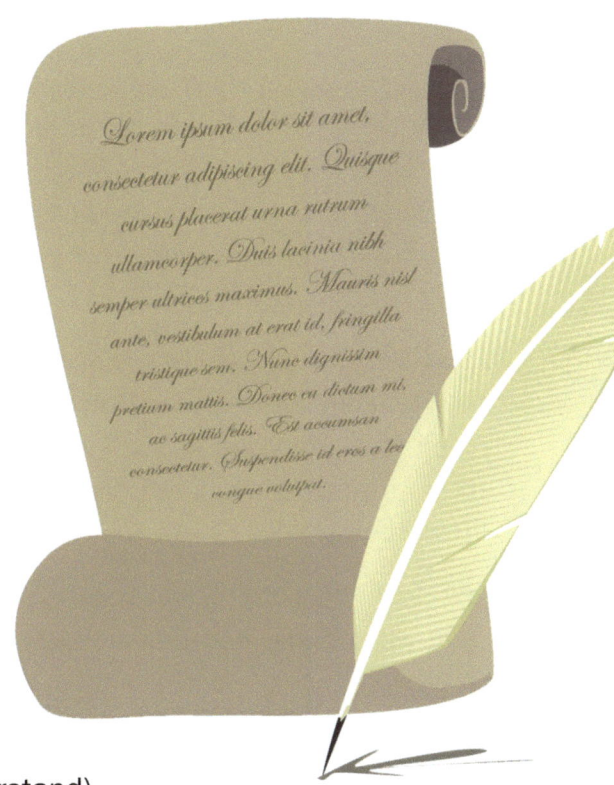

The Peace Treaty

One of Nani Serena's mission was to visit the Jews and Muslims. She wanted to know how they lived in peace and harmony alongside each other.

In her time frame she share her world with people from different beliefs and cultures. These differences in beliefs can give raise to many conflicts, most of the time inflamed by third parties. She wanted to find out how the newly appointed statesman, Prophet Muhammad (PBUH) manage these situations.

She once again found herself flying with her Star. They have been flying for awhile, sometimes even racing the birds. It was certainly a wonderful experience.

Serenestar pointed out to Nani Serena a large gathering. There seemed to be a discussion going on.

They started their descent to join these people. It was what Nani had thought.

They were drafting the **Constitution of Medina** which is a document written to maintain peace and co-operation among all the people living in Medina.

The document was written on something that looked like perhaps dried sheepskin. Two men were holding it up whilst another two were going to hammer it into a stone wall.

Nani Serena although invisible started mingling with the people.

They were the Ansars(helpers) and the emigrants from Mecca. The Meccans were thanking the Ansars for all the help they gave them, as when they arrived in Medina, they had nothing. They were praising the prophet for uniting them into this brotherhood only bonded by their beliefs.

She saw the Jews. She recognised them by their hairstyle and dress code. They were expressing their joys. They are in such appreciation that the Prophet recognised them as **People of The Book**.

By now, the scroll was already mounted. How she wished she had her mobile phone to take a photo.

She studied the writings of the scroll and read it out aloud:

In the name of Allah, the compassionate, the merciful.

This is an agreement with Muhammad the prophet

It is an agreement between all communities of Madinah

This is an agreement between Muslims and non-Muslims

The Jews have their religion and the Muslims have theirs

The Muslims will respect the rights of the Jews.

They will protect them.

And the Jews will be loyal to the Muslims and fight by their side

In this way, all those who stay in Madinah will be one community

Madinah shall be a sanctuary for the people of this document

If there is any misunderstanding

The Final judges shall be the prophet (PBUH)

And Allah

But this document will protect only just and honest people

It will not protect unjust people

Allah is the protector of the good

Allah is the protector of the God-fearing

And Muhammad (PBUH) is the messenger of Allah

The people were happy because they were all guaranteed their rights. Both Muslims and non-Muslims were told how to live together, and in peace.

Nani knew then what verse 256 of Surah Baqarah meant:

256. *Let there be no compulsion in religion: Truth stands out clear from Error: whoever rejects evil and believes in Allah hath grasped the most trustworthy hand-hold, that never breaks. And Allah heareth and knoweth all things.*

Change of the Qibla

Nani Serena wanted to accomplish so much in this mission before she gets taken back to earth.

Surah Baqarah talks about the change of the Qibla. She wanted to be there when it all happened.

Serenestar must find that time span for Nani Serena.

They have been flying for some time now and it was dawn. It was time for fajir. They came to a Mosque. The holy Prophet Muhammed (SAW) was leading a congregation of people in prayer. They were facing Masjid Al Aqsa.

In another area, the Jews were also in prayer and also facing Masjid Al Aqsa.

This has got to be it. They are finally there.

It was indeed a lovely experience for Nani Serena to witness.

When the prophet lived in Mecca, it was possible to face both the Kaaba and Masjid Aqsa when he prayed. But in Medina this was impossible. When he faced Masjid Al Aqsa his back was facing the Kaaba. This made him incredibly sad. The Kaaba was built by his ancestor Prophet Ibrahim (PBUH). He felt that he is not showing his due respect by turning his back to it. But he never complained to Allah.

He will just look up to the sky in sadness.

But something was about to change. This day he was invited to the house for a meal by one of his companions, Bishr b. Bara'b. Ma'rur.

When the time of zuhr prayer came, the Prophet rose to lead it. He had completed two rak'ahs and was in the third when he received the revelation:

We have certainly seen the turning of your face, [O Muhammad], toward the heaven, and We will surely turn you to a qiblah with which you will be pleased. So turn your face toward al-Masjid al-haram. And wherever you [believers] are, turn your faces toward it [in prayer]. Indeed, those

Nani Serena joined the Umah of Prophet Muhammad (PBUH)

who have been given the Scripture well know that it is the truth from their Lord. And Allah is not unaware of what they do. ***(2:144)***

The direction of the Qibla has now been changed. There was a proclamation of this change and from then until today, and to the end of the world Muslims will face the Kabaa as their direction of praying.

Nani Serena was so pleased that she was a witness to this.

Building of the Kabaa

And [mention] when We made the House a place of return for the people and [a place of] security. And take, [O believers], from the standing place of Abraham a place of prayer. And We charged Abraham and Ishmael, [saying], "Purify My House for those who perform Tawaf and those who are staying [there] for worship and those who bow and prostrate [in prayer]." ***(2:125)***

Nani Serena is familiar with the above revelation and felt that she must be taken back in time to watch it all happening.

Serenestar is certainly granting all of Nani's wishes and is more than happy to take her there.

This will indeed be an exceedingly long journey. Prophet Ibrahim (PBUH) lived an awfully long time ago.

However, Nani Serena is looking forward to this journey. She likes the freedom of travelling in space.

Up in the sky, something did not feel right. She felt a feeling of discomfort. There was something different about this night.

Zooming through the sky, they were really having to dodge like what seems to be fallen stars. There were many. The sky seemed ablaze with them.

Serenestar was to tell Nani an interesting story.

She said that Allah swt explained this in the holy Quran.

"And We have guarded it (the heavens) from every accursed devil, except one who is able to snatch a hearing and he is pursued by a brightly burning flame." (Quran **15:17-18**)

Serenestar said that Allah swt is explaining here about the flying Jinns. Jinns are also Allah's creations and were created for the same purpose as humans, to worship Allah. There are three types of Jinns, and the ones tonight are the flying type. Jinns are very much like humans. Some are believers and some non-believers.

The Jinns they are seeing tonight are certainly not good jinns. They are flying beneath the lower heavens to listen to the Angels conversing amongst themselves. They are talking about future events which they heard from Allah. This information, the flying jinns will transfer to the fortune-tellers. This is a great sin in Islam.

This practice is not allowed, and they get shot at.

We see them as shooting stars.

Finally, Nani Serena and her star entered another time zone. The dark night suddenly disappeared and gave rise to the bright shining sun. They appeared to be in a desert.

As they were descending, they could see some figures. There were an older man and a young boy about 30ish.

Nani screamed!

She recognised them as Prophet Ibraheem and his son Ishmael, may peace and blessings of Allah be upon them.

They were now in Makkah.

They were between the hills of Safa and Marwa.

Nani Serena is witnessing the building of the Kaaba by Prophet Ibraheem (AS) and his son Ishmael (AS).

Nani wanted to rush and give them her salaams and thank them for this structure that unite all Muslims in their prayers. But of course, she cannot do that. She is a time traveller and invisible. All she could do is just stand there in awe and wonder, watching the Kaaba being built.

Prophet Ibraheem seemed to be standing on a stone to build the Kabaa and his son was passing the bricks to him. As the walls of the Kabaa was getting higher that stone was rising too. Nani Serena could see an imprint of the prophet's footprints. It then dawned on her that would later come to be known as the **Maqame** Ibraheem.

All of Nani Serena's wish had come through, but she is not ready to return to Planet Earth yet. She wanted to remain on Jupiter. She must wait for her grandkids to take them back safely to their beds in their own galaxy.

Serenestar agreed and suggested she will use this opportunity in her extended stay to discuss Surah Baqarah further.

Once again Nani Serena and her companion are flying in the Milky Way. Nani is getting quite good at this now and can fly independently. With arms outstretched, flapping like a bird, Nani is having the time of her life.

Many of the stars now recognise Nani Serena and sends their salaams and kisses, as she zooms pass them.

They finally arrived in Jupiter, and nicely settled at Serenestar's home.

Private Moments with Nani Serena and Serenestar

Nani Serena will use her extended stay in Jupiter to learn more about the message of Surah Baqarah from Serenestar.

Serenestar held Nani Serena's hand and in the most sympathetic voice she looked into Nani's eyes and started to speak to her:

"Nani Serena you have seen the wonders of Allah's creations, you have visited the people of the past. Allah did not create you and all of this in vain. You just do not live and become extinct after death. There is a hereafter where you will be judged for your actions".

Nani Serena was very touched by those opening lines and sat there transfixed listening to her Star.

She explained that our life did not begin at birth but long before that, and that when Allah created Prophet Aadam(AS) all the souls of everyone who will ever exist were created.

Serenestar continued to inform that Allah swt introduced himself to the souls and then wiped that memory out; placing each soul to make the journey on earth for an appointed time.

They then talked about the guidance verses in Surah Baqarah which is all making sense now to Nani Serena.

This is the Sharia Law that is very much mis understood by Non-Muslims. These laws are intended to give a clear path to live in a civilised society, representing the ultimate manifestation of the divine mercy.

The Legal Rulings of the Shariah Law regulates all human actions. There are the forbidden actions of consuming alcohol, engaging in usury, gambling.

There are laws relating to personal acts of worship, laws relating to commercial dealings, laws relating to marriage and divorce, and penal laws

All these laws and rulings ensure the preservation of human life. *Serenestar explained the following verse in Surah Baqarah*

And when it is said to them, "Follow what Allah has revealed," they say, "Rather, we will follow that which we found our fathers doing." Even though their fathers understood nothing, nor were they guided? [2:170]

Nani Serena's Star explained that this verse refers to following the customs of our ancestors blindly, rather than looking for guidance from Quran and the sunnah of Prophet Muhammed (PBUH). She advised that the way of truth is only gained by wisdom and revelation and we must not follow the customs of our ancestors without any rationale proof.

She ensured that Nani understood that this verse is not only referring to the pagans in Arabia but also to us present day.

One aspect that Nani Serena was not familiar with was about the last two verses of Surah Baqarah:

285. *The Messenger believeth in what hath been revealed to him from his Lord, as do the men of faith. Each one (of them) believeth in Allah, His angels, His books, and His apostles. "We make no distinction (they say) between one and another of His apostles." And they say: "We hear, and we obey: (We seek) Thy forgiveness, our Lord, and to Thee is the end of all journeys."*

286. *On no soul doth Allah Place a burden greater than it can bear. It gets every good that it earns, and it suffers every ill that it earns. (Pray:) "Our Lord! Condemn us not if we forget or fall into error; our Lord! Lay not on us a burden Like that which Thou didst lay on those before us; Our Lord! Lay not on us a burden greater than we have strength to bear. Blot out our sins, and grant us forgiveness. Have mercy on us. Thou art our Protector; Help us against those who stand against faith."*

Serenestar told Nani that these verses were revealed directly to Prophet Muhammed (PBUH) during his accension to heaven and if offers protection from the Shaitaan.

They then talked about the other protection Surah found in Surah Baqarah, Ayatul Khursi.

Nani will use the remainder of her time reflecting on this journey and educate others when returned to earth.

It was Serenestar.

She was addressing everyone. She told that in the beginning there was just one ball in the universe. There was no sun, no moon, no stars. This ball, because of the intense heat, grew larger and larger, until there was a big explosion with lots of smoke.

And the solar system was formed from this occurrence.

Allah then created seven heavens one above the other.

She then went on to talk about Surah Baqarah.

She tells them that the surah contains many rules on a variety of topics guiding how to live on this earth. It explains why Allah created jinns and mankind and what will happen when they die.

She went on to say that Allah sent many prophets to deliver these messages and Surah Baqarah contains information about most of these prophets and the times they lived in.

Serenestar then put a proposal out and asked if everyone would like their Star to take them back in time so they can receive these messages with the people of those times.

Nani Serena and her grandchildren could not believe what they were hearing and shouted their agreement in chorus.

Each gave an account of which time they would like to be transported to.

Nani Serena wanted to be taken back in time to the Umah of the Holy Prophet Muhammed (PBUH) after his second Hijrah to Medina.

Layla chose to visit the time when Prophet Aadam (PBUH) was created in the lower heaven.

Keyaan wanted to time travel in the era of Pharaoh and Prophet Musa (PBUH).

Jasmine wanted to find out why the Surah was called Surah Baqarah (The Cow) and asked her star to take her to that period.

Omari is going to live in the era of Prophet Dawood (PBUH) and Jalut.